The Woman Downstairs

THE WOMAN DOWNSTAIRS
Julie Bruck

Brick Books

CANADIAN CATALOGUING IN PUBLICATION DATA

Bruck, Julie, 1957-
The woman downstairs

Poems.
ISBN 0-919626-66-1

I. Title.

PS8553.R83W66 1993   C811'.54   C93-094901-3
PR9199.3.B78W66 1993

The support of the Canada Council and the Ontario Arts
Council is gratefully acknowledged. The support of the
Government of Ontario through the Ministry of Culture,
Tourism and Recreation is also gratefully acknowledged.

Cover art by Lauren Schaffer. Author photo
by Peter Martin.

Typeset in Gill Sans, printed and bound by The Porcupine's
Quill. The stock is acid-free Zephyr Antique laid.

Brick Books
Box 38, Station B
London, Ontario
N6A 4V3

In memory of Kitty Hamilton:
Such an elemental gift.

Contents

III. SECOND SUN

No more romance
When the hunger's gone.
    – *Kate & Anna McGarrigle*

... now bounded, now immeasurable,
it is alternately stone in you and star.
    – *Rainer Maria Rilke*

I. AGAINST GLASS

Car Alarm

Outside the bank, a Mercedes Benz tells one
in a group of teenage boys he's *too close
to the vehicle. Please step back.* He does, and the car
says, *Thank you.* A bolder boy decides

to press things – rubs his thigh against the vehicle:
The car says, *You have stepped inside
the perimeter. Step back* – but some girls
have gathered, so the boy crosses his arms, stays

right where he is. The car starts to count down
from five. The boy doesn't move. *Thank you,*
says the car at zero, and the boy turns, gouges
the metallic finish with a key, while another

kicks the tires, and a third jumps on the hood.
All the while the car says, *You are too close
to the vehicle. Please step back.* The girls
scatter. The boys follow – a straggler twists

the antenna. *Thank you,* says the car. *Thank you.
Thank you.* A woman comes out of the bank
and looks crazily around. Someone she hasn't seen
in years, someone with a great patience, whom she may

have dreamed of last night or loved at seventeen;
someone she knows and can't quite place, has spoken.
Just now. Here in the street. This is the first thing
in a long time, of which she is certain.

The Bathrobe

Before dawn, the neighbours' conversation cuts into dreams,
carries into all the apartments from our shared courtyard.
A woman on a balcony is watching a man pack his car.
Here, she says, clutching a fistful of silky, blue fabric,
take this too, Billy, and flings down what billows into a bathrobe,
wafting on air with full sleeves – then she drops the sash.
Behind windows, the sleep-stained faces of my neighbours
wash up against glass: in the dim light their features
are smudged. Each of us is half-awake, each thinks the moment
is intensely private. Only the woman will go back to sleep,
bereft or satisfied, it's hard to say. We can shut our eyes
tight, as the man accelerates on the 401, but it's no use:
the sun snakes around the curtains, warms his left hand
on the wheel, ignites the blue acetate in his right.

I-80 West

In your favourite picture of you and me,
we're like a soft-drink commercial –
wind in hair, sun on surfaces, open
as the road, gulping down the miles,
each day bluer than the one before.
I keep it in the glove compartment:
the light this far west
would eat through it like bleach,
light that leaches in everywhere, tumbles now
through this restaurant window.

Three days away from you:
I'm getting used to being
a woman alone.
A bus-load of Rotarians just pulled out,
a faint smell of cedar,
like history in their wake.
Across the room, a young family.
The man keeps looking up,
while his wife in a shirtwaist dress
reads the menu to their child.
I try to imagine what's familiar between them,
the known scent of the child's neck,
blue barrettes on either side of her head,
while he eyes me, a woman not much younger
than the wife beside him, who may
have thickened with the years, care
of a small daughter. He seems to like
a woman alone, the one in the picture, say, laughing,
her head thrown back at impossible angles,
casting out losses like cigarette butts
from a moving car, hugging
the slick, hard surface of the road.

If it's freedom he sees here, he can have it.
I'll hand it to him like something on a plate.
He can take the car, cut circles
in the restaurant parking-lot like a cowboy,
roar back into this postcard of a morning,
one too cloudless for history or need,
track the odometer, steadily rising
into thinner air with the cool independence
I thought I was made of, the kind
that clears out commitment
like so many breakfast crumbs,
with a practiced sweep of the hand.

Sudden Heat

Three black women trade easy laughter,
their white charges in strollers still immobilized
with blankets. A postman slings his bag over one
shoulder, waves to the face in a third-storey window,
begins a wobbly aria. We have lived through
a long, dirty winter for this: now the Acura Legends
take their cell-phones off the hook. For just
one day, commuters grow giddy, miss their exits,
while the couple who have lived apart scramble
from their rusting Camaro, lay an old blanket
in some damp, secluded ditch and make love
the way they did when they first met – urgent
and surprised: By the roadside, their car radio
croons to the air, both doors flung wide.

To a Concerned Friend on Friday Afternoon

'Rilke here from six-o'clock on, reading to me.'
    – *Lou Andreas-Salomé*

Actually, I have a guest: Rilke, that
pale traveller is still here. No, I'll concede,
it's not ideal, but he expects little, doesn't
tie up the phone, and because he won't eat
I never worry about what gets cold and dry.

We have no shared history, you see,
aren't braided like family, that constant
disentangling, pulling and tearing of hair.
He's long since lost interest in sex;
sure, he reads old letters from Nietzsche's
girlfriend Lou, but since she's long gone
there's nothing to be done, and since my dreams
blend the men I've known into one composite,
we have more than a little in common.

Like most accidental celibates
we have nasty moments: Rilke
has a habit of quoting himself. He started
tonight, as the paperboy came to collect
and was counting change. Rainer came zooming
down the hall, fixed him with those icy blue eyes
shouting, 'don't you know *yet*'?
The kid, shy even at the best of times,
dropped his hole-punch and ran.
I never got the change.

He'll go in the end, he always does,
back to that castle, where the umlauts rattle.
And since these days I'm feeling a little
stiff myself, I might conjure him up from time
to time, when there's nothing on TV:
a sort of communion or reunion. Yes,
he *is* dead, friend, I think I'm entertaining
Rilke this weekend, and maybe you're right
to worry, but I have other delusions:
one's that this is temporary; that my life
awaits; that I can learn some useful things
from this guy who doesn't mess up the towels –
hell, he doesn't even *use* towels, and that if I got
a better offer tomorrow, a living one, I'd accept.

Solos for Cat, Toaster, Owl & Voice

Across the airshaft, the neighbours have raised
their kitchen window, placed a toaster on the ledge
with just enough room for their yellow-eyed cat
to do his own arranging. On Wednesday, he moved
the toaster left. Thursday, he pushed it back. Today,
he's tipped it over; charred slits stare north
and a long, black electric cord hangs alluringly down.

The concert pianist who lives below, a survivor
of Dachau who some nights opens his windows
and cries out into the airshaft, has tied a stuffed owl
to his clothesline, meant to scare off pigeons.
The cat can't see the owl, just paws at the toaster,
creeps along his ledge. The owl swivels as if motorized,
and I'm so struck by a vision of airborne, small appliances
I lean too far out. Startled, the cat looks up, toaster

flies four storeys. The owl pivots, undisturbed, steady
as a metronome. From the pianist's room come operatic
first notes, a woman's voice warms up. *Like this*,
I hear him say, as the cat reappears in the window,
Try it like this. The cat looks straight across the airshaft,
he stretches on his ledge, I place both hands
on mine. A melody rises. The owl keeps time.

The Woman Downstairs Used To Be Beautiful

This summer she's grown huge, a ham with legs,
she lumbers below, watering the garden with a hose.
From my balcony, the evening light seems kind
to the extra flesh, soft
on her print shift, the scarf that holds back
her dark hair, and for once I want to believe
she's not unhappy, not stuffing her face
to fill in the distance between her
and the unusually thin husband who travels, not hiding
in the body of the proverbial fat woman,
passed in the street without notice.
Instead, that she wants to be of consequence,
clearly visible to her small son stationed
on their balcony, that he never lose sight of such a broad floral back,
think she might leave him, vanish in the leaves below.
But the wail that comes from him's a thin, unwavering cry,
as if he never comes up for air, this wordless child's siren
of *come back, not enough, too far,* that has brought me
and, gradually, other neighbours onto our balconies
to look first on a small boy, who, thirty years from now
will turn his life over, say: *there was always
too much of her, she swallowed me up* – and then down
on a fat woman, breathlessly bending.

I Was Married to an Astronaut

I sang like a bird, he wanted to fly.
Practicing after work, over there –
by the window, on clear nights
I almost catch a glimpse of him, tethered
to the mothership, blinking on and off
in his baby-blue spacesuit like a star.

Those nights, I practice extra long –
he's shown me what comes of hard work.
In the window glass I could almost
be a Piaf or a Dietrich, many say
I've got the right lips.

I purr soft through the slow parts,
like cooing to a baby, but when I raise my arms,
I can go through the roof.
That's when I wish the neighbours
would knock or something – I'm half-way
to the moon. They should hear this.

The Goldfish

For Thomas Lux

Sometimes I'm scared I'll be buried alive, watching
these people through the cheap, flawed glass.
They're riveted to earthquake reports; claw-footed
bathtubs falling from hotel-rooms into streets,
building façades peeled back.
They seem to like things a little inverted – love
a hurricane, how the weatherman says
it will *slam* here, *slam* there, and they rock
in their chairs as if to music.

They're proud to be Canadians, specialists
in the barely imaginable, known for daring rescues
in planes named for moose, a certain facility
with fallen wires. So tonight, snug and warm,
they did seem let down when the big storm
lost strength; they went dull-eyed, lethargic
in the living-room.

They need only look out at their darkened yard:
rain has blown their scarecrow down, the hat
they gave it is blocks away, careening on the wind.
Or they might look closer at their sleeping son:
he is not what they think, all youth
and innocence. When they're away, he tortures
the pets, pulls hairs from the cat, takes me
from my bowl in his hot little fist, to see just how long
I'm good for in air. I try to lie flat and glistening,
don't squirm, struggle, or give him any action – I know
how short his attention span is, that he'll soon
lose interest in something so small, go back
to the TV's flicker and boom.

Not until those lights stop beaming in here
like lasers (my lidless eyes), and the room is dark
and quiet, except for the rain which falls like rain,
can I sink to the bottom and rest my fins:
I know to move at the first sound of life, lest
they mistake me for dead-in-the-night, and neat
to the point of negligence, dispose of me too soon.

I've seen those alligators on the six-o-clock news,
the kind who surface every few years, snout-first
in somebody's toilet. How people love
the snaggle-toothed surprise – love my green brother best
just before they flush him back down – and straggle in
for newstime's exact counts and numbers, to see
who got sucked under when the big one hit.

Dayniter

Inside the Toronto-Montreal train,
a dark-haired woman drags her suitcase down the aisle.
From where I sit, she appears life-sized,
but when she steps into the rainy night,
under the sign that reads, *Cornwall*,
she's greeted by two tiny parents.
The tiny Dad grabs her large suitcase –
it must be so heavy! – and she follows,
towering over them in her voluminous down coat,
like some terrible freak duckling.

All through Ontario, I see this scene repeated.
Big lugs, like linebackers on steroids, put on
their *Queen's Engineering* jackets, step out
into home-with-the-folks-for-Christmas, suddenly
gross. Where will the parents put them
in such tiny houses, tiny beds? They'll stoop
to enter their childhood rooms, accidentally
crush the family dog. But each time they trail
the shrunken couples to cars in the adjacent lots,
just before the train pulls out, as they're talking –
parents appraising them or announcing what's for dinner –
the giants are bending to their tiny parents,
already becoming smaller.

II. METHODS FOR FALLING

Triad

These May weeks are blinding,
the seasonal dazzle of the city
and you coming to me. It's all
in the course of a life, I tell myself,
even when the apartment buzzer sends me flying
to the door to meet you – someone else's
known, level quantity – always the same
puzzled face peering up the stairwell:
of course you can come up, I call.

Weeks of afternoons and arms, our bodies
knit beside the bright window, sounds
of commerce rising from the street,
while above us, departing flights
criss-cross the homecomers,
sun on their wings.
After you've gone home, I watch the jets:
how steady they seem, like dirigibles
moving on their numbered paths, one right,
one left, leaving empty for a moment
what the window frames as sky –

Where's the retinal damage
a good friend said this could bring?
The risk of blue invitation seems
apart from this life,
a plain square of colour
and of so little interest
without its figures, like this room
where we touch, and go.

Ribcage

I keep the ribcage under wraps.
It feigns satisfaction all day,
filled with breath and nourishment;
it is an exemplary ribcage in the ballet studio.
Look, I say to my group of senior citizens,
*just lift, as if someone is pulling you
slowly to one side.*
And it detaches itself
and dances its ribcage dance.

I put it to bed nights, filled, tucked in.
It rises and falls, slowly, evenly,
but if wakened suddenly, 4 a.m.,
the heart jangling inside tin ribs,
in an uproar from dreams
or sirens or sounds at the door –
it wakens hollow, empty,
a catcher's mitt of bone.

One lit window, 5 a.m.,
the chest is anchored.
A solitary bus rattles,
empty, down the street;
a metal jack-o-lantern,
moving through darkness thick as water.
The ribcage tautens, strains,
dreams of lurching down the avenue.

Try it.
Just lift.

News of a Move

Your father, she writes, *is impossible.*
Five minutes in a paint store, so many colours,
and he looks like he's going to explode.

I'm a thousand miles away, bargaining
with shadows, with possibility, always
on the threshold of some promised definition.

How must it feel to move again,
new apartment, choices of flooring and counter-tops?
To consider now, the heights of appliances,

bad backs and ease of access — and when
all that's done, what's it like to think
of this as a life's final move?

Against the winter sky, same gray
as my mother's stationery, bare branches
seem to rain down to the ground.

It's small, she's written in her tiny black script,
but that's what we needed, the kind of place
we could close around us.

Conservation

Since your mother spent a lifetime
listing, folding, and caring for her things,
and you won't have them given away in garbage bags,
we wrap eleven cream-soup bowls,
nine bread and butter, tea service
for eight with seven saucers,
carefully itemize everything:
tape the boxes tight.

Today, her dressing table was the last load
for two stocky Peruvian movers.
It stood on the pavement, legs
curved and fragile, its mirror
folded in on itself, till they hoisted
it up and slammed the van door –
it was efficient, we smack of efficiency.

Her death was a dispersal.
We're still folding, wrapping,
putting things away.
Nothing with monograms,
nothing with stains, the things
we keep have value.
They appreciate.

Approaches

We separated at the airport,
each of us bound for a different city, a friend
wearing a grief so palpable it pulsed
just below the surface of her skin.
Her father had died, and for days
others circled her, protecting,
but also vying for a glimpse of themselves
in the sad green pools her eyes had become.
The funeral's in Florida, both
of our planes left from separate gates:
she to attend an absence while I fly home,
imagining loss from under the shadow of living parents,
who follow, like storm-birds, my life.
How many times have I dreamed their deaths and failures?

At the gate, in a long, white-hooded sweater,
my friend looked incongruous, like a shepherd.
Now her plane must be banking towards the Everglades –
I put a cold drink in her hand – the glass sweats
against her palm, but I can't quite find
the weight of her legs, or remember her shoes well enough
to root them to the carpet, how she feels
when she finally stands.
She's arriving to bury an absence
just as my flight bears down on the runway, turns
and taxis toward the lit terminal,
catapulted almost home.

Closure

Who hasn't had days when the door
stayed ajar; the important business call
in which you meant to sound brisk
but goodbye came out *bye-bye*?
Or when you talked over someone
saying what they've tried for years
to say; hung up in the middle
of *I love you*, or got hung up on.
A plane takes off and a small child
turns from the cloud-streaked
window, asks, *what happened?*,
and sobs for the rest of the trip.
Poof! – gone are her grandfather's
delicate nose-hairs, the sunlit world
with its parking-lot demarcations.
There's just this terrible shaking
between the past and future.
You want to know when it stops.

Connection

My parents have noticed each other
after forty years;
my father gets up from his chair,
nuzzles my mother at the kitchen sink.

Lately, he's taken to buying her pastries.
Ask for bread, she says,
he brings home the bakery.
She opens the boxes, beaming,
arranges the cakes on a plate.
I don't know what to do with this happy couple,
who eat so heartily and ski for miles.

I plug my car into their weekends.
Mountain air and early nights
renew my childhood like the taste
of some long-forgotten food.

Nothing is good, my mother taught me.
The displays at the bakery
only look that way, so by association
did men, so did I.

Nothing is good or good enough
but this place,
where I keep my things near the door,
begin packing as soon as I arrive,
and sleep soundly.

Voices carry in their woods.
I'm always waiting
for them to catch up, straining
for the sound of ski-poles, coming through the trees.
Now, gauging the distance of their laughter
I grow restless in the brilliant light,
push off down the trail.

Now my going's no longer a betrayal,
just car exhaust on Sunday nights,
my parents reading in their lit interior.
See you later, says my father,
blooming like a hot-house flower
in the glow of my mother's lamp.

I start my small car,
a loaf of her bread beside me on the seat,
drive the access roads with the radio loud.
Joining the string of tail-lights,
I lose sight of the house on the hill,
where the small betrayals don't seem to matter
and I don't know what does.

One day I'll forget to unplug the block-heater,
drive away and pull the house down.
In the rear-view mirror, the mountains, sky,
the whole gourmet display
will tumble and break apart,
becoming light as confetti
thrown at a wedding,
a fistful of coloured ash.

93 North

Too modern, you said to the books I'd brought with me,
songs that I knew how to sing.
At twenty-nine, you've written off the century,
so gracious in your ordered house.

Cousins, we wear our shared histories
so differently. The woman you live with
came and went in pressed slacks,
your conversations muted as the colour of her hair.

We took out a map of Russia last night,
found our grandparents' town.
Somewhere between Minsk and Pinsk
you kept saying and laughing,
and when you found *Shumsk*,
were suddenly sober.

The months just go, you said in August,
each day bright as a child's pail and shovel.
You'd planned to travel, but the afternoons accumulate,
stack up at your door like newspapers.
At least I can keep the desires intact, you said
and I turned the talk to childhood.

On the Interstate, families are sealed in
with beach chairs and coolers,
trappings of a summer almost spent.
Where the traffic slows for roadwork,
bulldozers rear up like circus elephants
as the flag man patiently waves us on.

At a café up the road,
the woman at the next table
tells the man she's with,
there's no relationship.
It's not you, she says, *it could be anyone,*
and besides, you've never even seen me in the morning,
as he chases an olive in his empty glass,
feet dumb under the table.

All these bodies, crossing and turning
and heading north:
every route on the map is red or blue,
ribbons through fields of corn, drowsy on their stalks.
Mill towns and villages, all glinting whites:
sedate hands on the town-hall clocks;
School street, *Oak* street, *Church* street, the season
spills from the roadside stands.
New England summer draws over us like a blanket:
we grope under cover, before the days become cool again,
blue and acute.

✻ ✻ ✻

We become a continuum of tail-lights at dusk,
while the radio sings something about a happy idiot.
A man hauls a garden hose across his lawn, reports
from the beaches say record crowds.
Let's dance, Colonel, says the child on a billboard
to a box of Kentucky-fried.

So close to home and here too,
the night is thick with crickets:
even the parking-lot near your house
sang all summer.
I hope your doors are open now,
your restless cat's free to stalk the garden:
you're right, *time flies,*
and like the road in the rear-view mirror,
everything recedes.
But if each town's a point of light,
falling away,
the road map still cradles their luminous names,
unspoken, alive in the dark.

Litany Against Sense

After you'd spoken your piece, tried compromise,
planned your escape, baked a cake, worked things through,
with your breath restored to normal;
after you'd left the empty rooms
in perfect order, the note
written in the tight little hand;

after you'd gotten the cab driver to wait,
didn't seduce him but collected the clothes,
paper bags, rotten suitcase bound with cord,
and made it, despite rumours of street gangs,
safely to the lit interior;
after you'd reached the elevator, arms laden,

pressed the right button to take you
to the right floor, your sense of accomplishment
a warm thing spreading up from your feet, doors close on cue,
and nothing happens, nothing but the rush of blood in your ears
and a voice comes out of the elevator shaft, saying
now you're so sane, be reasonable.

Snakes & Wrenches

Now that you're gone I'm efficient.
I'm getting good at the details, the way
one learns to ride a horse, and seeing
to things that we'd put off, today, the plumber,
his specialized snakes and wrenches.
I sit on the rim of the tub, watch the furred hand
grip the side of the porcelain sink, wrench the pipes open,
and loose all that muck on the bathroom floor.

Hair, he says, indicating, *dental floss in there too,*
as if he'd fished you whole from that pipe:
I sit here as I did on dark winter mornings,
teasing your attentions to hair and teeth,
your lathered face joking back in the steamy mirror,
both of us laughing in this narrow little room
we called our temporary tropic – now spinning
on its axis – how easily the plumber's back
could be yours, as he pokes at our mingled hairs.

There's a method to falling, I was taught once
by a pro: how to fly clear of split rail and hoof, biding
that interminable lapse from the time you know it's happening
till the ground comes up to meet you and takes your breath away.
For a time in the air you think you can tumble
forever, seeing the world as if for the first time:
such a world of difference between you and your shadow,
kicking and screaming on the unforgiving ground.

Kampuchea by the Weekend

One letter from Bangkok, the next from Hanoi.
For months you keep moving, and I follow
in dreams: straw huts, river barges,
this open-air restaurant by the sea.

We've just started to talk when an old Lao man
puts his lunch on a nearby, sloping table.
One by one, he releases each dish: they crash
to the floor – first rice, then fish and tea.

He launches the chopsticks last, lights
a cigarette, crosses his legs and arms, exhales,
sinks into the spindly chair like someone
who has eaten well, has finished.

We've barely talked, now we're laughing
too hard – embarrassed by the strange, small rebellion,
and a chopstick rolling steadily our way.
It's so old – this zen pivot from the body, from

attachment – and taking in your fine profile,
I know this is how I'll last see you: a boat leaves,
you'll be on it. Nothing will get broken
or thrown. I can't will you back.

III. SECOND SUN

Incendiary

Spring arrived this morning
like an alarm. The old man passed
my window at the usual time, past
kids smoking outside the Tabagie,
their fluorescent jackets flung
on the sidewalk or tied around their hips.
I grabbed a sweater, headed for the street,
around streams of run-off, and followed
two high-school boys who, looking back
to make sure they were seen, tossed
lit matches through a chain-link fence
where a derelict slept in the sun.
Nothing burned, and I followed them
downhill on their incendiary path,
carefully, because I have this tendency
to trip and I have places to go; a wallet
full of important papers; a temporary
phone number for an impossible love
to whom I have said no all winter,
tempered to maybe, and now,
in the absence of pleasure or pain,
say yes — because there comes a time
when you want to live as dangerously
as all the other citizens — to love
and be loved just as hard, and hurt.

Wake

If I look hard enough
there are cities in my wake:
a million lit windows
in the lake's deep green.
They tremble at each stroke I take,
the picture falls apart,
then comes back into focus.

Four floors up, our kitchen windows
faced each other.
Lights off nights, I watched him
drink at the kitchen table,
forearm stretched along the sill,
as she moved, a background,
and the child, asleep.
This normalcy was what
I measured my life against.

A panel truck came and went.
She must have taken the child
when she left, his girlfriend
put up curtains.
The picture falls apart.
Panel truck and a pale child
standing on the curb.

I turn to the bright geometry of a rowboat
moored at the dock, the cabin
now a matchbox at the end of the lake.

Panel truck, child,
pale on the curb.

The wind is up.
Swim back.

House Sitter, 4 a.m.

Pool-hopping, says the younger cop,
Used to do it myself, as a kid.
I stare past the blur of uniform, across
the dimly-lit lawn: two plastic garden chairs bob
in the shallow end – drawn close, conversant.

All night I've listened to laughter,
to the sleek glissando of furtive swimmers.
I felt ridiculous, alone in the house, keyed
to every sound, finally phoning the cops
from inside a locked bathroom, then cruising
room to room like a watchful cat.

Now the porch light burns. The absent owner's cat
digs in his litter: each grain of sand flies
with the pitch and force of flung glass. Glass house;
invisible swimmers who scale six-foot fences.

They must be asleep by now, spooned
around each other, hair still damp on the sheets –
or maybe they've moved a few blocks down, lie seal-like
on the beach, dreaming, inches from the tide.

The pool's circulating pump sends water
over the edge, as I go barefoot on wet grass,
kneel and angle for the chairs. In water,
they're so heavy – resistant as bodies. For a second
I even see hair billow out, as I haul the last one in,
I am *that* tired, *that* sick with desire.

Suppose

We were both supposed to be somewhere else,
the afternoon my brakes failed, I steered us
safely to the local mechanic and we left
the car ticking, dripping in his lot.

We were supposed to be somewhere else,
all that hot afternoon, while around
the small house, cicadas roared,
sprinklers went on and off with timers.

We were supposed to be somewhere else
that evening when, freshly showered,
dressed, we paid the mechanic,
and I drove you to the train, watched

you recede to where you were supposed
to be. I drove back to the empty house,
and the brakes responded just like
they were supposed to. You once

described your single act of heroism:
a car with two small kids started rolling
into traffic. You ran alongside, grabbed
the hand-brake and all the kids could say

was, *please, mister, put us back*
where we're supposed to be.
Back at the house, I held the car key
tightly in my hand. I thought

we could run all the lights, gun it
for New Zealand, bright scarves
snapping in the wind. Suppose
we roared right out of our lives

and just kept going? Even if
we'd crashed – the car, a smoking
wreck – who'd care? We were
supposed to emerge, unscathed.

Stone's Throw

In early light, an overpass on The Cross-Bronx
proclaims, *I love André !* in turquoise paint.
At eighty-miles-an-hour, it seems a stone's throw
from the beach town I've left, through Cairo, Peru,
and Paradox, New York – to Schroon Lake,
where the whole town's been purchased
by *The World of Life*, and each building lists
a Board of Directors: Jack someone and two others.

The news says King Hussein is east of here, making his way
to Kennebunkport, while at home on the Pont Mercier,
a young soldier spits at an armed Mohawk warrior.
A great deal of sighing before one of them
howls, *I'm not going to kill you at all.*

At the local grocery I inquire about *The World of Life*.
A religious group, says a pale young woman in line.
What kind?, I ask. *We're non-denominational*, she says,
indicating the boyfriend with Triumph tattoos.
And I'm driving again, past *The World of Life*,
where someone's flung a towel on an Adirondack chair,
and blonde people stroll the fenced-in grounds.

Last night at dusk, I watched the tide go out,
the lifeguard's chair stretch its shadow on the sand.
A couple passed. She was talking about birthing centers:
The baby's born underwater, you know? *Uh-huh*, he said,
touching the small of her back, while an hour away,
someone sprayed buoyant capitals in the fading light
with care and an exclamation point.

This is what I need when I think of stones
thrown at random from highway bridges, that
involuntary flinch as I take the Northway home:
south of where army and natives fume
in identical flak jackets, beyond *The World of Life,*
and west of where a man's hand is a bridge
when it meets the hollow of a woman's back –
someone loves André, permanently in blue.

Timing Your Run

Philippe Laheurte (1957-1991)

The night before there was a break-in at your store.
There was an afternoon when the lock had been fixed,
and you said you'd drop an extra key at Laurent's place
after work. There was a call from your wife. All day,
you'd waited to run, but just as you went out,
it really started pouring. You were like a little boy
in the rain, Albert Mah said, and you came back drenched,
pleased with your time. There was a pair of New Balance
trainers for a customer with narrow feet, the rain
on the shoulders of the UPS man who waited
while you signed. A tuna sandwich made for you
at the dépanneur next door. Your thin fingers
on the brown paper bag. There was a blue car.
There was what you said about this run of bad luck –
robberies at the store, a fire on New Year's Day, about
training for a comeback in the fall, believing everything
could turn around. How happy the woman with long,
narrow feet was when you called to say her shoes
were in. There was your hand, hours after dark, slipping
the extra key through Laurent's mail slot, Laurent asleep.
There was a car coming. The key lay on the floor all night.
After running you'd showered in the store's tiny bathroom.
There was the bar of soap, still wet. There was a blue car
slicing a corner. There was your black car, stopped
at the light. There was Laurent, awake in the morning,
a freshly-cut key on the cool floor. There is tonight's
news footage of you winning races, explaining
the difference between two kinds of heel cups,
bending a shoe as you speak. There was the key
you wanted Laurent to have in case something
happened. There is Laurent, half-asleep, picking it up.

Reprints

For Duane Michals

A friend's call says, *you've got to see*
the pictures of last summer, how they
caught that time, and I can hardly wait
for those green and blue-hued rectangles
with their strong, polished faces.
They'll grin through winter from fridge doors,
office boards: friends with their arms draped
around each other's necks; parents
with youth restored, holding each other
so tight they seem locked; Philip's long body
cradled by the hammock. Each summer seems
like something dreamed, each followed
by a greater string – do I need to list them? – of losses.
Where I live is lined with these photos,
everyone in them kissed by sun and water,
safe and loved for the last good time. *See?*
We were happy once. This is my proof.

Still Life

When you give a gift, there is momentum,
and the weight shifts from body to body.
　　　　　– Lewis Hyde

Alone at dawn, walking the ridge,
I raised an arm to stretch sleep from it.
She seemed to float into the clearing,
this pale runner, framed in the crook of my arm.
The slap of her shoes – the kind designed
for the serious athlete – seemed too loud
on the wet grass to announce her joined bones,
their thin sheath of skin. The rigid shoes
seemed to do the running, propelled
the familiar figure past and into the woods – my old self,
glimpsed and gone – leaving my legs twitching
to burn heat from my body before morning
could sear mist from the ridge.

But I turned then, walked slowly down the hill,
remembering the runner at the edge of the woods,
caught like a deer in a rifle's sight.
The light on her seemed cold and static,
but it caught her appraising eye, which swivelled
in its defined socket, and stared right back.

I was hungry: there were apples waiting in my room,
a friend's gift from the night before
when they'd seemed too waxen and perfect
to take from their bowl. I took one,
then another, ate them all,
even their cores, until I felt their sweetness
rise in my throat like a debt.

I know what it is to have a hunger so deep
you don't even try to fill it.
Deprive the body and, yes, it's true,
the world becomes more beautiful, colours
take on hues seen only in memory,
other people – light years away.
Just now, the sun cut a swathe across the floor,
climbed into the expanse of my lap.
It will take great effort to stand, retrieve
my shoes, and walk out to join the others,
dragging this ambivalence, this weight.
Fool, she whispers, running in place,
you could have been all eyes.
I shut the door gently, not exactly in homage –
she does what she can, and she does it well.
I shut the door softly, with respect.

Summer on Rewind

A man and a woman walk backwards
from opposite directions, turn and meet
on a corner, while emergency vehicles scream
across 34th Street, against the one-way signs.
Their embrace lasts so long the homeless
back off, withdraw their cracked palms.
A small car takes them up the Thruway,
trunk-first. Although she appears
to be driving, both stare at the receding
skyline like riders in a caboose.
They shimmy from the car, lunch hurtles
from their mouths, rearranges itself
on plates; wine flows into a bottle,
sealed with original cork, metal closure.
A waitress takes everything away.
In the middle of a lake, they tread water,
laughing and kissing, lips losing their blue.
They swim in feet-first on their stomachs;
toes begin a perfect arc and they're upright
on the dock, towels reattached to dry bodies.
Sleep ends in exhaustion, figures weaving
on a narrow bed; buttons are fastened
with pleasure. They're bright-eyed, shot
through with energy as a second man stands
between them holding a drink, indicating
one to the other. Each withdraws a hand,
each toddles backwards. She goes to her
parked car, repacks a suitcase. A friend's
sedan swallows him, backs down the road.
It is morning. It is night. It is the day
before and the lake is a pane of glass.

Then, a small disturbance by the dock:
a circle of ripples contracts, as a hawk
drops its small fish and travels tail-first,
up into the clear blue on a backwards path
so clean, so purposeful it seems each talon,
each muscle, each fragile bone wants
nothing but to hunger, higher, alone.

Cautious

We've done this for years, walked streets
like we're lovers, dangled current heartbreaks
in a tone of constant complaint. By now,
I've grown used to your visits' colours:
how brilliant the city looks when you hold
a ticket out of it, how *temporary* trots behind us,
dog on a leash.

This morning we walked past the ex-Premier's
house, pavement still steaming from early rain.
The door opened and there he was – with a tall
young woman, one ripe tomato in each of her hands.
She jogged up the street, juggling the fruit
with consummate skill, you and I
speechless as the blur of red receded.

On the way to the airport, you still sound amazed:
Montreal seems a place where *anything's possible,*
those tomatoes were so red.
On this strip of fast-food joints, which to me
had always seemed like anywhere, we drive through a spring storm
sunny on one side, pouring on the other, a rainbow
arcs the boulevard, marries Pizza Hut to Mr. Muffler
and your plane leaves right on time.

We don't dance on park benches
in the city I drive home to: there aren't
enough jobs here, for ten months of the year
we're numb as stored suitcases – all winter long,
we barely look out. That woman you loved
was too old (or young), wouldn't move (she might),
from this city you'd taken to calling Venus for its visions
and beautiful women – distinct from the Midwest,
which must be Earth, where love is seen
in a harder light, something built to endure.

Why must longing be our greatest pleasure, banked
for vacation time, an interlude, a lapse?
Henceforth, tomatoes return to the salad bars
of steakhouse chains with head offices in the Midwest,
and if I still see a rainbow over the road, I'll call it
a fluke of hot air and timing, extraordinary
chemical event – don't look for long,
or pleasure may be what we come to expect: a city
of jugglers and bright red globes, where you catch one,
hold it, watch it ripen in your hand.

Who We Are Now

The man who runs the parking lot at St. Hubert & Duluth
holds our keys in one closed hand, curses this country
with the other. *In Soviet Union, I am doctor, like Chekhov –*
his fifth identity in the last six months. *Here I clean hospital*
after midnight. You must pick up keys by eleven.

My friends plan their lives in a nearby Greek restaurant:
plans subject to jobs, lovers, children, or lack of same –
most of all, this constant gnawing at who we are,
exactly what we're supposed to be doing here.
After the meal, the wine, strong Greek coffee,
a ballpoint meanders on the paper tablecloth, variations
on the same story – each year, less embellishment.

I have seen him wave off customers he didn't like the look of:
In Greece, I am anthropologist – he barks, shaking his fist
at a blue Chevette that has backed out in search of a meter.
Quebec people are racist – Canadians are worse. I do not think,
he says, squinting at us, *that you are pure Canadian.*

When we finally head home in our reclaimed vehicles,
it is always early April, always snowing, always unseasonal.
We huddle in the glow of the car's dials and gauges, stare
into the red light at Cherrier like some kind of second sun,
longing for sleep, for dreams to redeem us.

I am Armenian, he states proudly, *and this place is dead.*
In Moscow, my cousin has fourteen fruit stores.
He thrusts the wrong keys at us, I point to the correct hook.
East Europe is living. Next year, I sell antibiotics in Bucharest.
Good business, he says, releasing our keys. *Good night.*

Acknowledgements

My thanks to the editors of the following publications in which versions of these poems first appear or are forthcoming:

The Malahat Review – Still Life, The Woman Downstairs Used To Be Beautiful, House Sitter, 4 a.m., Cautious, Reprints, Timing Your Run, Snakes & Wrenches, Stone's Throw, Kampuchea by the Weekend, The Goldfish, Summer on Rewind. *New Virginia Review* – Car Alarm. *Event* – Conservation. *Denver Quarterly & Celebrating Canadian Women* (Fitzhenry & Whiteside) – Connection. *The New Yorker* – Who We Are Now. *The Randall Jarrell Poetry Prize* – Summer on Rewind. *errata* – To a Concerned Friend on Friday Afternoon, Incendiary.

Thanks also to:

The Explorations Program of the Canada Council & the MacDowell Colony for the gift of time. The Tuesday Night Group & the MFA Program at Warren Wilson College. Ellen Bryant Voigt, Martha Collins, and everyone at Brick for their help in shaping the manuscript. Mark Abley, Bill Dodge, Cornelius Eady, Nina & the late Bill Finkelstein, Joe Fiorito, Robert Fulford, Michael Harris, Michele Landsberg, Susan Meisner, Rita Schaffer, Philip Szporer, Heather Wallace and Joel Yanofsky, for their encouragement and support. My parents, Nina and Gerald Bruck, in whose lives things get made and matter.

Julie Bruck lives in Montreal, where she works as an arts publicist. She has an MFA from the Warren Wilson Program for Writers, in North Carolina, and her poems have appeared in such magazines as *The Malahat Review, Denver Quarterly* and *The New Yorker.* She was a finalist for a 1992 National Magazine Award, and has had recent grants and fellowships from the Canada Council and the MacDowell Colony. *The Woman Downstairs* is her first book.